Word on the street

Ridiculous things we've overheard in **London**

#wordonthestreet

Published by Time Out
4th Floor
125 Shaftesbury Avenue
London WC2H 8AD
Tel: + 44 (0)20 7813 3000
Email: guides@timeout.com
www.timeout.com

© Time Out Group Ltd
Chairman & Founder Tony Elliott
Chief Executive Officer Tim Arthur

Editor Alexi Duggins
Art Director Anthony Huggins
Production Controller Katie Mulhern-Bhudia
Editorial Director Sarah Guy
Senior Publishing Brand Manager Luthfa Begum
Proofreader John Watson

With special thanks to Ellen Wishart and Becky Redman

Time Out and the Time Out logo are trademarks of Time Out Group Ltd.

This edition first published in Great Britain in 2014 by Ebury Publishing
A Random House Group Company
Company information can be found on www.randomhouse.co.uk
Random House UK Limited Reg. No. 954009
10 9 8 7 6 5 4 3 2

For further distribution details, see www.timeout.com

ISBN: 978-1-84670-278-5

A CIP catalogue record for this book is available from the British Library.

Printed and bound by CPI Group (UK) Ltd, Croydon, CR0 4YY

Penguin Random House is committed to a sustainable future
for our business, our readers and our planet. This book is
made from Forest Stewardship Council® certified paper.

Word on the street
The story

Since *Time Out* became a free magazine back in September 2012, we've been asked one question over and again. That question is this:

'You're bloody well making up those *Word on the street* quotes, aren't you?'

We've been asked it at parties. We've been asked it by our families. We've been asked it so often that after telling people where we work, it's tempting to squeal: 'We don't write them ourselves!' Which can be awkward if you were about to be asked, 'How do you come up with your articles?'

But hey, it's all due to *Word on the street's* popularity. Every week *Time Out's* Twitter account buzzes with love for it. People wander in to our office clutching jotted-down quotes. We've even had late-night voicemails from pubs, with readers slurrily keeping us at the cutting edge of nonsensical bar chat.

So we decided to collate the finest entries into one book. Thus bringing insights about cheeses with penises, peri peri otters and photos of people's bums to coffee tables across the capital. Alright, alright: toilets across the capital.

Oh, and to settle it once and for all: no, we don't make them up. We could never imitate the utter, nutty brilliance that Londoners come out with. Just turn the pages and see for yourselves.

Alexi Duggins

Word on the street
Contents

❼ Gourmet eating, London style

Aka 'Things you'll never hear on Masterchef.'

❽ They've got a point, though, haven't they?

It's funny 'cos it's true…

❾ Say WHAT?

If you know what these people are on about, please let us know.

❿ Oh, to have been a fly on the wall…

Amazing-sounding stories, told in one soundbite.

⓫ Liven up, grandma!

Things you say when you need to get out of the house more.

⓬ Too much information!

Seriously, skip this chapter if you're a sensitive soul.

⓭ Long day, eh?

Unnecessary aggression + a random overhearing = mucho chuckles.

⓮ Worst boast EVER

Leave it, mate: you're not impressing anyone.

⓯ Well, you can't fault their honesty

Not sure we'd have admitted these things in public, but hey…

⓰ Maybe you should rethink that one…

Misnomers, nonsense and plain, plain daftness.

⓱ Couples' drama

Ways you know your relationship is dead.

⓲ Weirdos, the lot of ya

An insight into the minds of London's oddballs.

1

Who said romance was dead?

The world's worst
seduction techniques.

'If you were a frog, I'd buy you a really nice tank.'

'I like your dress. The dots make me want to run my hands up and down it like it's Braille.'

'Hey, your stomach looks like a potato. No! In a good way!'

'I'm probably 95 per cent single at the moment.'

'It's a good job we know each other. I'm kind of stuck to your face.'

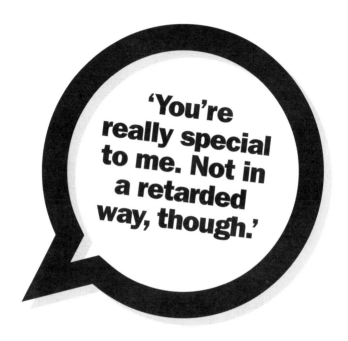

2

Who says Londoners aren't friendly?

Judging by these quotes, it's their mouths that say that.

‘You’re about as subtle as a fart in a bath.’

'Putting suncream on you is like rubbing custard into a carpet.'

'She drives like a turtle on heroin.'

WHO SAYS LONDONERS AREN'T FRIENDLY?

'You can tell she's a dickhead by her eyebrows.'

'Spending time with my family puts me off having kids. The world does not need more people like that.'

'And THAT, my friend, is exactly why people think you're a slag.'

'You see that guy with the ten-stone testicles? That's you, that is.'

'You're not sorry. The way British people use the words "sorry", "thank you" and "please" doesn't mean anything. They're practically commas.'

'I can taste how much you hate your job in my coffee. Can I have a fresh one with some love in it please?'

'She was blonde, slightly overweight and had a professional qualification: the kind you find in Clapham after the rugby.'

'I hope you drive better than you walk.'

'Mum, I do not want a screwdriver set for my 21st! Don't you DARE get me a screwdriver set!'

'If you're going to play the village idiot, at least have the decency to get a smock and a five-bar gate.'

3

21st-century problems

Or, as we like to think of it: 'Things that would baffle your grandparents'.

'I roll a tennis ball up the wall with my bottom cheek to relieve my sciatica.'

'No, don't TELL me where you are. Who does that nowadays? Text me a link.'

'All I'm saying is that she's the only one at baby yoga with cellulite.'

'I've sweated off all the glue from this tit tape.'

'Hold on, I need to think about this in relation to my personal fitness regime.'

'I had to walk 40 minutes to find a Waitrose that stocks tofu!'

'My keffiyeh totally lost its shape when I had it dry-cleaned.'

'My chiropractor says you have to find the right water for you.'

'I mean, who goes to Charleston lessons in a pink stretch Jeep?'

Life's big questions

The issues that are currently keeping Londoners awake at night.

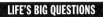

'Can boys get crabs? I thought they just crawled around the foof.'

'Is it wrong to send a man a photo of your anus that another man took?'

'What came first: the chicken or the hen?'

'If we don't have footage of dinosaurs, then how do we know they existed?'

'Dogs or cats: which are sexier?'

'Oi, Michael, you're good at science. If I'm coughing, does that mean I've got germs?'

'Is it still called dogging if it's on a coach?'

'Yeah, I know alopecia. Fourth member of Misteeq, right?'

Aw, bless...

Dopey but cute things
we've overheard in London.

'West Ham isn't short for West Hampstead? Are you sure?'

AW, BLESS...

'Ampersand: that's a type of lizard, no?'

'If your mum's got that illness where she's afraid to leave the house, does that mean she's homophobic?'

'Man, someone stole Nelson's hand! Right from the top of the column in Trafalgar Square!'

'San Francisco's a bit gay. It's like the Vauxhall of America.'

'You know what I really hate? I really hate it when I'm sad.'

'Lychees? What kind of cheese is that?'

'What's a clitoris? Is it that little bell thing?'

'Oh my God, how did they make that Nelson Mandela film so quickly after he died?'

'Is it just me, or does Will Smith look like that dude from "Fresh Prince"?'

AW, BLESS...

'Daddy, did Paul McCartney really let a baby drive his car?'

'How is your new dog? Oh, it's a cat.'

AW, BLESS…

'I wish I had more confidence with mushrooms.'

'It was so romantic: he made me rice with mashed potato!'

Deep truths

The quintessential wisdoms
of Londoners.

'Kids are like farts: you only like your own.'

'There is no "I" in "team", but "team IS "meat" spelled backwards.'

'Clearly, there's a reason nostrils are the same size as fingers.'

'Poo is always shit, but shit isn't always poo.'

'Yoga mats
are like STDs:
everyone gets one
at some stage.'

'Up is always
up and down is
always down.
Ooh! Unless
you're a bat!'

'You can't rate something by licking it.'

'More than two shakes and it's a wank.'

'In the office, nothing says you've got your shit together like a salmon-pink shirt.'

7

Gourmet eating, London style

Aka 'Things you'll never hear on "Masterchef".'

'If Nando's put peri peri on an otter, I'd eat it.'

'No fruit with bacon. That's my one rule!'

'Someone really needs to stop me eating Werther's Originals for breakfast.'

'I see the corner shop's started selling cock-flavoured noodles.'

'White bread
is like the ninja
of the food world.
It's a silent
killer.'

'I like toast.
You know
who else likes
toast? Elvis.'

'I lost so much weight when all I did was take drugs and eat McDonald's.'

'You KNOW I don't eat for 16 hours on a Tuesday!'

'Sausage trumps bacon. Everybody knows that.'

'Don't start on my Pot Noodle! What about them men that go up to space and have to eat dried apples and that?'

'It's 2013! Why does food still have calories?'

8

They've got a point, though, haven't they?

It's funny 'cos it's true…

'The Nobel Peace Prize. It's like the Oscars of peace, right?'

'Going to McDonald's for a salad is like going to a prostitute for a hug.'

'Within five years, there'll be a pop star who is literally just a vagina.'

'If the Death Star had a tube stop, it'd be Westminster.'

'You do know Tilda Swinton! She's that actress who looks like she's from the future!'

'Toilet paper's rubbish. Think about it: if you had shit on your face, you wouldn't wipe it off with a tissue.'

'Butterflies: they're just spiders with wings.'

'If you're going to play Candy Crush Saga in the loo at work, you should at least turn the sound off.'

'"The Great Gatsby" with a hip hop soundtrack? That's like doing the Bible on ice!'

'Being fancied by someone ugly is like winning Scottish Footballer of the Year.'

'Vintage nights are for girls who think that drinking cocktails out of teacups is fucking amazing.'

'Just renewed my annual rail season ticket. Talk about the Great Train Robbery!'

'We go out to find someone to stay in with, don't we?'

'You can't be a peaceful pirate. That's like being a celibate prostitute.'

9

Say WHAT?

If you know what these people are on about, please let us know.

'You need to mark your territory. Pee all over him like a dog.'

'Guys, I have an itchy boob: it's going to rain!'

'You don't slag off a man's AstroTurf when he's sitting right next to it.'

'I once ate dog biscuits. Was trying to turn myself into a dog.'

'She was fluent in hieroglyphics. I dunno how anyone can speak hieroglyphics. That is literally "bird mouse stick eye".'

'Is that my nipple? What on earth is it getting up to over there?'

'I didn't understand a word that aubergine was saying.'

'I hate burritos: they're racist.'

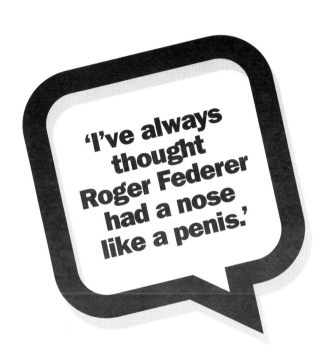

Oh, to have been a fly on the wall...

Amazing-sounding stories, told in one soundbite.

'I told him: "This hat is worth more than you earn." And then I kicked him in the dick.'

'That was the first and last time I used the word "dubstep" in the work environment...'

OH, TO HAVE BEEN A FLY ON THE WALL...

'It was the weirdest date ever. He kept spraying me with Dettol.'

'I tried berries and glycerine up my bum and that didn't work.'

'You know: it was that place. The one where you ordered a chicken burger and it had a snake in it.'

'Turns out I'd been saying: "I'm so horny I need a drink." Bloody exchange student never corrected me once.'

'I absolutely did not threaten to punch him. I threatened to stick popcorn up his arse.'

'He's got a horse mask on, he's got his cock out, he's pissing on my best friend.'

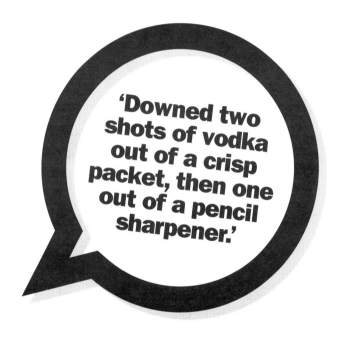

11

Liven up, grandma!

Things you say when you need to get out of the house more.

'I need more excitement in my life. I've got to get back into cross stitch.'

‘Me? Take drugs? I can’t even handle chickpeas.’

‘That’s a lovely fence.’

'I've got a really funny story for you about binary codes.'

'Oh man, it is ALL CHANGE in Aldi!'

'Since discovering Twinings teas, I've never looked back.'

'I love it when shit kicks off on "This Morning" '.

Too much information!

Seriously, skip this chapter
if you're a sensitive soul.

'He was so sweaty that his cock left an outline on the stool.'

'If I had a penis, I would totally wee in a bin.'

'She MUST have had an accident. It was all over her trousers.'

'I've just sweated a litre out of my crotch.'

'It was a great night. My bedspread looked like a Pollock painting by the end of it.'

'I just did a shit that was such hard work, I had to take my T-shirt off.'

'She reckons that she's got a "fladge": a flabby vag.'

'He kept putting glasses on his penis and pretending it was an old man.'

'We got the momentum all wrong. He grabbed my crotch and I farted in his face.'

13

Long day, eh?

Unnecessary aggression + a random overhearing = mucho chuckles.

'Bon Jovi! I'd rather masturbate into my own mouth!'

'Feet are disgusting. I'd rather have wheels.'

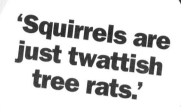

'Your hair is messier than Katie Price's personal life.'

'That's meant to be a drawing of a DOVE? Looks like a tooth with wings.'

'The French in London: it's not an invasion, it's an infestation.'

'Women are like fairground rides. They're all fucking mental.'

'I mean, BLONDE? It's not an adult's hair colour, is it?'

'I've never met anyone from outside London who actually knows what work is.'

'Trusting Americans is like trusting Louis Walsh on "The X Factor"'

'Glitter is a disease and it can't be stopped.'

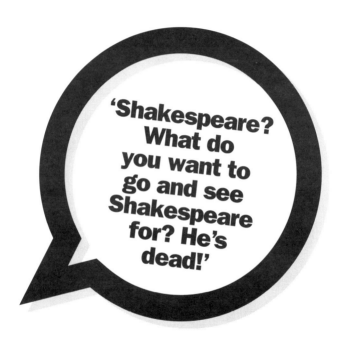

14

Worst boast EVER

Leave it, mate: you're
not impressing anyone.

'I just invented the jazz burp.'

‘My dad has watched a LOT of adult films.’

‘I think it’s the moisturiser I use: I can stick stuff to my face all day long!’

'I sing a lot of powerful ballads in the shower.'

'Of course, I made him clean the toilet before I threw up in it.'

'I got a cock grind off Calvin Harris. BEFORE he was famous.'

'Seriously, look at my beard. If John Peel wasn't dead, I could be a lookalike.'

'I'm so old, I used to throw sheep on Facebook.'

'The whole day was a whirlwind of romance and rugby.'

'My phone is so old, it pre-dates both my marriage AND my divorce.'

'I do have a really clear concept of groins. Shit has HAPPENED to my groin.'

Well, you can't fault their honesty

Not sure we'd have admitted these things in public, but hey…

WELL, YOU CAN'T FAULT THEIR HONESTY

'That horse looks like me in my profile picture.'

'He won't want to poke me. I look like my brother tonight.'

'Texted her a photo of my forearm. She thought it was my penis. She's gonna be so disappointed.'

'I'm Jewish AND ginger, so fuck you!'

'He said, "Marry me." And I said, "You're funny, mate." Seriously, I just laughed in his face.'

'I've got nipples like coat hangers.'

'My vagina has shut down through sheer disappointment.'

'To cut a long story short: I fingered my boss.'

16

Maybe you should rethink that one...

Misnomers, nonsense and plain, plain daftness.

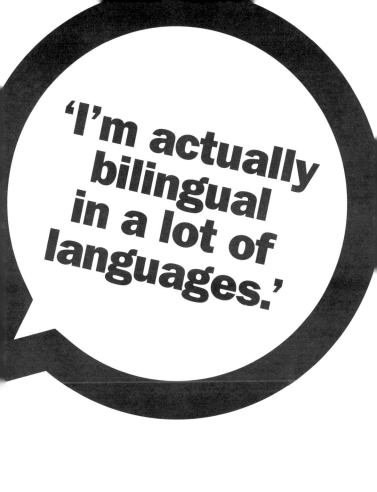

'Yes, I know where Bath is! It's in Bristol.'

'The Bible is the largest work of fiction since "Lord of the Rings".'

'She's half Chinese, half Singaporean, half Italian and half English.'

'Stop questioning me! What is this, the Spanish Armada?'

'Thirty minutes? That's almost half an hour!'

'Go get a dictionary: "oak" is spelt "O-K-E". Oke.'

MAYBE YOU SHOULD RETHINK THAT ONE...

'That new Zadie Smith book: is the intro just a load of sentences?'

'The thing about him is that he hates feelings with a passion.'

'London IS a country, stupid. It's surrounded by the Thames.'

'I know this town like the back of my head.'

'Let's do it like they do on the History channel.'

'Tom Daley is so annoying. He's like the male version of Justin Bieber.'

17

Couples' drama

Ways you know your
relationship is dead.

‘Not only were you equivocating, you were equivocating while you were inside me.’

'Sure, I eat cold beans from the can, but you're the one who collects their nail clippings.'

'I don't care WHAT Jim says Rebecca does on his birthday. It ain't happening.'

'We were about to have sex, but then I checked my bank account. From that point it all went wrong.'

'Afterwards, I feel a little lonely, even though she's still there.'

'Of course it's a compliment! I wouldn't do just anyone's mum!'

'I can't believe you brought your sex sofa with you.'

'Please stop taking our 12-year-old son to topless bars.'

'It always hurts my feelings when you laugh at my clothes.'

Weirdos, the lot of ya

An insight into the minds of London's oddballs.

‘Do you remember when I had that Gypsy curse?’

'You've clearly never sniffed a teenager's sheets.'

'One of the things I think is under-rated is the back view of my penis.'

'I've not been able to look at David Hasselhoff since that sex dream.'

'I flipped through my notebook and there was just a picture of a face... bleeding.'

'She's got no right to be angry with me. I've hooked her up with loads of guys since ditching her.'

'That was the night in Reigate when Alan was crying, wasn't it? That was a great night!'

Heard on the street?

Have your ears rejoiced to the sound of a brilliant quote you think we should know about?

Tweet us @timeoutlondon, with the hashtag #wordonthestreet.

Or, for hundreds more brilliant things we've overheard in London, go to www.timeout.com/wots

Word on the street

Ridiculous things we've overheard in **London**

#wordonthestreet